# #Leadwell

## A collection of leadership thoughts for thoughtful leaders.

## Michael Holland

Bishop House Consulting
INCORPORATED

ISBN 978-0-9848893-5-8

*Now all glory to God, who is able, through his mighty power at work within us, to accomplish infinitely more than we might ask or think.*

*Ephesians 3:20 (NLT)*

# Table of Contents

# Introduction

Great leaders leverage opportunities to create deep self-awareness of their personal leadership style and build cohesive teams through trusted relationships. The *Leadership Learning Moments* contained in this book will prompt leaders at all levels of maturity to think about their leadership style, their relationships, and the impact they could have within their organization.

As you read through these pages, take the time to reflect on your core management behavior, and consider the ways you could tweak your leadership habits to become more effective.

*Lead Well!*

Michael Holland
Founder/President, Bishop House Consulting, Inc.

#Leadwell

# Personal Leadership

# Style

#Leadwell

# Why You Should Understand Your Leadership Style

Your leadership style is a melting pot of your personality, your life experiences, your natural/preferred communication style, the level of your emotional intelligence, and your perspective. The success of both young leaders and well-seasoned leaders in eliciting the willing collaboration of others toward a worthwhile goal depends heavily on the capability of these leaders to be self-actualized. In other words, how well does a leader know their style, and how well can they adjust their style to meet the demands of moment?

Knowing your leadership style enables you to be successful in these three key areas.

**Enabling Relationship Margin** – Superficial relationships with employees are easy, but there is little relationship margin (the space, latitude, and time offered to you from a trusted relationship). Understanding both how you react and how others perceive your reaction to pressure, delegation, conflict, stress, and success creates a relationship margin. This margin of a split second to several seconds buys you the time to read the situation and appropriately adjust your style.

**Creating and Sustaining Momentum** – First, fully understand how and why your momentum fluctuates. Then, seek to understand how you de-motivate others, both intentionally and unintentionally. Your goal is to reach a level of self-actualization where you understand how you can motivate others both directly and through the leaders who may work for you.

**Building Leadership Maturity** – Immature leaders act. Mature leaders think, act, and reflect. Mature leaders gather intelligence from

5

all interactions – even boring meetings – to add to their understanding of human dynamics. Mature leaders have high emotional intelligence: they are socially aware enough to self-manage themselves so that they can build strong relationships.

As you mature, so will other leaders around you, and thus you will help to raise the leadership capacity of the organization.

**Coaching Thoughts – For You and Your Peers**

- What are some of your natural leadership tendencies? Make a list of some of the characteristics that define you as a leader.

- Why do you think that understanding your natural leadership tendencies will help you in the three areas mentioned here? Can you think of any other benefits of understanding your leadership style?

# What's Your K-Cup Management Style?

This morning, I brewed a fresh cup of coffee on our Keurig brewer, as I have done many times before. As I watched the coffee trickle into my cup, I began to think about all the different flavors of coffee that are available. In many offices today, you have access to these single-shot coffee brewers and the attitude-adjusting properties of the various flavors. For example: what mood might "Emeril's Big Easy Bold" inspire? Next time you're grabbing a K-cup, stop and think about the flavor you're choosing and how it could "magically" impact your attitude.

- **Breakfast Blend** – Getting business done, having consistent conversations in meetings and with employees. Perfect for that morning huddle or weekly staff meeting.

- **French Vanilla** – Pull back to escape a bit of the crazy day. See the warmer side of situations and employee interactions. Great for those weekly feedback sessions.

- **Dark Magic Extra Bold** – Turn up the volume! Your 1:30 pm, post-food coma wake-up call before you start work on next year's budget, or as you prepare for the reviewing the 127-slide onboarding PowerPoint deck HR wants you to review.

- **Chocolate Glazed Donut** – It's your Friday mid-morning prep for the brainstorming meeting on creative staffing solutions. Or the late afternoon "cup of joe" to bring along on your one-on-one walking update meeting outside with an employee.

- **Decaf French Roast** – Slow down, you're moving too fast for your team. Gain the deep, rich taste for deep, rich thoughts without the overstimulation and eye-twitching caffeine high that scares your employees away.

As a manager, you should be thinking about adjusting your attitude, persona, perspective every time you prepare to meet with an employee or attend a meeting. Coffee flavors and strengths can help to temporarily adjust the chemical reactions in your body and thus help you to adjust your attitude. But the real change comes from your "thinking ahead" to what type of attitude, persona, or perspective you'll need to adopt. The coffee is simply a routine to help the behavior be a bit more sticky in your life.

## Coaching Thoughts – For You and Your Peers

- Which "coffee flavor" fits with your natural style? Are you more of a Dark Magic Extra Bold, or a Decaf French Roast? What about your employees? If your styles don't match, you might want to think about trying a different flavor when you interact with them.

- We act differently around different people: to some extent, that comes naturally. Think back over the past week. What are some times when could have used that extra "boost"? Were there certain situations/individuals that needed less caffeine than others?

- Choosing different coffee flavors depending on the situation you are facing serves as a concrete (and admit it, fun) reminder that you can't use the same attitude with every person. What are some other areas where you could use a similar reminder? Take a few moments to brainstorm for solutions (grounded in concrete, positive actions, like the coffee flavor one) to those personal issues.

# He's Not Really Evil

Solving difficult problems and making wise organizational decisions can tax even the most self-actualized, mature, enlightened, and cohesive leadership team. A key to success is the capability to **assume positive intent** from the others on your team. This means that when the tight-fisted CFO shoots down your proposal because the costs involved are too high, and you immediately feel the adrenaline jolt and desire to rattle off the dozen or so successful business altering proposals you've put forward over the years that he's always said were too expensive, you maturely fight back the urge to react. More importantly, you sincerely strive to listen more intently to his comments, thoughts, and opinions. You engage with the CFO, asking open-ended questions to gain full insight on what he sees and knows. Others engage in the lively debate, and the discussion culminates in a well-vetted decision all can support.

Wow, like that happens every day in the meetings you're in with peer leaders in the organization!

Assuming positive intent is a behavior that must be practiced in order to be mastered: pushing down your initial reactions and biases to allow your mind to open up and fully hear the peer leader – or employee – with whom you are talking does not come easily. Reflecting upon how you interact and draw out conversations will reveal opportunities to improve. Doing this enables you to make better decisions personally, and will help you to enable a team or organization to work more cohesively to make better decisions.

Our leadership model is predicated upon the belief that leaders at all levels must constantly reflect upon how their personal leadership style enables their leadership behaviors and the building of trusted relationships. One of the most difficult aspects of this self-reflection

9

process is to wipe away the biases and get rid of the baggage that we accumulate through each day "on the job" so that we can see, with clarity, the full impact of ourselves on the relationships. To do this, we must:

- Discern how our natural leadership and communication style might make us disinclined to hear well. If you've been through a great DiSC® training, look back at your Everything DiSC® profile and how you can better understand and work with those with other styles.

- Change the cadence and tone of our questions and comments to enable conversations rather than talking heads yelling past each other. As per Stephen Covey's Habit #5, "Seek first to understand, then to be understood".

- We must believe – again and again and again – that the peer leader or boss or employee is not evil. In fact, they are more likely just like you. And you both likely believe in God, since 92% of Americans say they believe in God. Find common ground from which you can build your relationship.

You're an adult, so you get to decide how you will invest your energy. Just know that positive energy brings tremendously higher returns on investment than negative energy.

## Coaching Thoughts – For You and Your Peers

- What does the phrase "assume positive intent" mean to you? After taking a moment to define it in your own words, write it on a Post-It note and stick it somewhere you'll see it often so that you can be reminded to see the best in others.

- Is assuming positive intent something that can only benefit workplace conversations and situations? For what other occasions might this be a good tool?

- So you've decided to make a point to see the best in others and give them the benefit of the doubt. How can you encourage the people on your team to do the same?

# The Celery Test of Your Leadership

While at the grocery store, you see two friends checking out with different cashiers. One is buying nachos, French opinion dip, a 12-pack of Coke, and a box of pastries. The other friend is buying fresh celery, low-fat yogurt, bananas, and organic apple juice. Both friends have recently told you that living a healthier life is very important to them. Clearly, one friend has aligned his actions with what he says he believes.

Your leadership decisions and behaviors reveal your true beliefs, purpose, and what's most important to you. Many leaders talk a good game about how they lead, inspire, and motivate their employees, but only a few self-actualized, hearty leaders actually lead in ways that support what they say. The evidence for this is striking when you see their employees:

- Empowered employees will surround a leader who empowers others.

- Confident employees will surround a leader who has instilled confidence in others.

- Energized employees will surround a leader who has inspired others to a great cause.

If you're buying celery and healthy foods, you don't need to tell me you're trying to live a healthy life: I'll already know that you are. The same goes for living out good leadership. If you are wondering where the good leaders are in your company, just find the pockets of highly engaged, energized, and empowered employees: they will point you directly to the better leaders.

## Coaching Thoughts – For You and Your Peers

- Take a few minutes to look at the leaders in your life: do they pass the celery test? Now do the same for yourself: do you?

- What beliefs form the core of your leadership principles? How do they shape the way you treat your employees, peers, and bosses?

#Leadwell

# Work of Leaders

#Leadwell

# Balancing the Work of Leaders

The Wright Brothers were successful in inventing and building the first controlled airplane even though they were neither as wealthy nor as educated as their rivals (neither brother received a high school diploma). But what they did have was a clear vision, an undying belief, and the capability to align and unify their resources to execute extremely well. This is what we affectionately call leadership.

Leaders often struggle with success because they don't fully grasp how they themselves are the dynamic in the environment they are attempting to influence. They underestimate both the impact and the limitations of their natural leadership style on their energy and behavior throughout the life cycle of vision to alignment to execution.

**Vision**, in its simplest form, is an imagined future state. A vision provides your team with purpose, and guides the development of goals, decision making, and the potential to unify your team. Some of us are naturals at visioning— leveraging optimism and big thinking to be bold in our exploration of what could be. Others struggle with the weight of reality, limiting the potential of boldness.

**Aligning resources** is the opposite of directing and delegating. Leaders often believe that when their team is delivering work and being productive, the team is aligned with the leader and the vision. But employees work diligently because they are paid to work, while aligned followers engage in work because they believe in the obtainability of the future state. When a leader has invested in enabling an open communication process that provides clarity and generates enthusiasm, then the all-important buy-in occurs. Are you a patient leader who can develop enthusiasm and collaborative engagement? Or did that last question make you want to stop reading?

**Execution** is making the vision come to reality through the aligned resources. Effective execution results from your work enabling and motivating your followers through well-thought-out structures and plans, and from providing continuous, critical feedback on progress. Driving action is important. But you must balance this drive with effective feedback cycles.

So the question you should be asking yourself today is this: is your team following you, or merely working for you?

**Coaching Thoughts – For You and Your Peers**

- Do you find yourself more likely to underestimate your impact as a leader, or your limitations?

- Which of the three points (Vision, Aligning Resources, or Execution) comes most naturally to you? Which is most difficult? How can you work to improve in that area?

# Modeling Good Management Techniques

Manager Matt sits at the small table outside a coffee shop enjoying the fresh air and the aroma of coffee. He's waiting for Erin, one of his employees, to arrive. It's time to deliver her yearly performance review. Matt relishes the opportunity to have this climatic yearly conversation because he's prepared, he's already delivered the key messages to Erin throughout the year, and he knows how to have this conversation. Ten years earlier, Super Boss Barbara had taught Manager Matt how to deliver feedback. In fact, Barbara didn't just teach Matt, she showed and modeled it for him.

Manager Matt thinks back to the methodology Super Boss Barbara used and how he's used the same structure throughout his years. It seems so simple.

- **You Watch Me Do** – Super Boss Barbara had Manager Matt shadow her as she delivered feedback to an employee. Afterwards, the two managers debriefed on the session, discussing what worked what could have been better. They talked through the process, and she explained to Matt why she said what she said, and how she anticipated the tone of the conversation.

- **We Do Together** – Barbara and Matt prepared together for a feedback discussion with an employee. Then they delivered the feedback to the employee together. Afterwards, the two managers debriefed on the session, again discussing what worked and what could have been better.

- **I Watch You As You Do** – Matt prepared for an employee feedback session and Barbara shadowed Matt as he delivered the session. Afterwards, the two managers debriefed on the session.

- **You Teach Someone Else To Do** – Matt came alongside a brand new manager and mentored the manager, using the same process to guide him. (Teaching someone else what you've learned cements the learning into your behaviors.) Afterwards, Matt went to Barbara and the two managers once again discussed what worked in the session and what could have been better.

Have you had a Super Boss Barbara in your life? Are you one in someone else's? It's never too late to start doing the right things to be a good manager and help others to become good managers.

**Coaching Thoughts – For You and Your Peers**

- After each step in Super Boss Barbara's method in delivering feedback, she and Manager Matt debrief. Is this necessary, or is it a place to cut corners? What might happen if you *didn't* take the time after each session to figure out what worked and what could have been better?

- This model for providing feedback relies heavily on learning by example. If Barbara would have simply told Matt how to do it instead of showing him, would she have saved time in the short term? Would the training have been as effective in the long run? Take a moment to think about this, and imagine the possible consequences of a lesser investment in Matt's training.

- The structure Barbara uses for performance review is important, but there are several other key pieces. Re-read the first paragraph. What are the first two pieces to delivering good feedback?

o   What are some ways in which you can prepare for delivering a performance review?

o   Have you made it a point to provide key messages to each of your employees throughout the year?

# Management 101

Your role as a leader – should you choose to accept it – is to effectively manage the people asset you've been charged with owning. This means:

1. You are responsible and accountable for the effectiveness and productivity of each individual person on your team, as well as the team as a whole.

2. You have a title, but you need to earn the right to lead. Sure, people will do what you say because they have to, but that's all they will do. To elicit greater dedication you must earn the right to lead.

3. You make more money because you have a greater responsibility... not because you're entitled to the money to make the car payments on that new Audi you just bought.

4. While you write and deliver performance reviews because HR told you to, your real role is to be delivering constant feedback to employees. A performance review is a bureaucratic weapon used by corporations to force managers to do the work they should be doing every day.

5. You have to stop using the words "they" and "them" for management because you are they and them.

6. Your job is to ask those awkward questions that no one else wants to in order to bring key issues and conflicts to the surface. Plus, you can really get to know your employees.

7.  Accountability is no longer a nifty term you get to throw around. You are fully accountable for all the good things and challenging things your employees do.

8.  You will sit in meetings that seem to be, and likely are, totally useless, and you will receive more emails than are humanly possible to read during a work day.

But most importantly, you will have the opportunity to influence the lives of people whose whole perspective –of a day or even a season of life—can be changed for the better by the way in which you choose to lead.

**Coaching Thoughts – For You and Your Peers**

- Is there one point (or even two or more) on this list that you find yourself struggling with? Are there some that come more naturally to you?

- Why is it important to recognize that these come along with being a leader? Can you be a good leader without them?

- Pick something from this list to focus on this week, and make a conscious effort to improve your leadership in this area.

# Building a Cohesive Team

During a recent visit to Lake Placid, I was able to see the USA Hockey Team's Miracle on Ice exhibit. What an exhilarating time, seeing the pictures and watching a replay of that magical game! Without much knowledge, we'd think this team just happened to come together and play their hearts out at a critical moment to win the greatest game on ice for the USA. But like all great teams, there was intense pain and agony in the building of the "team." This building takes investment, struggle, curiosity, intrigue, and in the end, some blood, sweat, and tears.

Patrick Lencioni provides a great model to help us see the ingredients required to build a cohesive team. In his famous book, *The Five Dysfunctions of a Team: A Leadership Fable,* and his most recent book, *The Advantage*, Lencioni clearly articulates the recipe to follow.

**Build Foundations of Trust** – Be vulnerable to a level which is uncomfortable, and allow yourself the freedom to develop relationships that allow for and require honesty, compassion and forgiveness. Yes, you will have to forgive some people… often, more than once.

**Master Conflict** – Leverage these trusted relationships to pursue truth and optimal decision-making. Healthy conflict draws out real debate and constructive analysis, which provides for real time permission to fire. The key is unemotional, unfiltered, issue-driven discussion.

**Achieve Commitment** – If people don't weigh in on decisions, they don't buy into decisions, no matter how hard they shake their heads. Great teams thrive not on consensus but on full commitment to decisions, which comes after healthy, constructive debate. Unfortunately, too many leaders have learned the art of passive agreement.

**Embrace Accountability** – Have the courage to confront and be confronted, because you and your peers have together committed deeply to decisions. Imagine a relationship with a peer executive that is so solid you can call him out for missing a major deliverable that the team had committed to… and he thanks you for it.

**Focus on Results** – Team is #1. The collective results are more important than any individual's. You are thrilled with the team's results (even when they are not directly because of you) because you are part of the team.

Invest 136 minutes and $1.99 to rent the Miracle on Ice movie. Watch for the tipping points when the team moves through the building blocks outlined above. And watch the very last minutes of the film as the team captain, standing alone on the gold medal winner's podium, can't stay alone because he knows that Team is #1.

**Coaching Thoughts – For You and Your Peers**

- What is the feel of the teams of which you are a part? Are your successes "miracles", or do all the team members follow the recipe above?

- Which of the ingredients in the recipe comes the hardest to you? What can you do to improve your abilities in that area?

# Do One Thing Each Day

About four months into their new role, young leaders struggle as they hit their tipping point with the realization that they have all this "management stuff" to do and they still have "real work" to do. They are executing the same behaviors and habits learned from years as an individual contributor and expecting different results. Mature leaders find themselves in the same situation when they're suddenly offered the opportunity to take on a special project or small functional team.

How is it that some leaders know how to roll with the change in work load?

Our counsel to leaders . . . do one thing each day in the new role or new situation. A small task, an additional conversation, a follow-up phone call, a walk to say hello, an arrival at work 7 minutes earlier. Just do one thing every day, 5 days a week for 250 work days in the next year. Just do one thing and your water dripping focus will not only reduce the size of the boulders you feel piled upon you but also will eventually create the behaviors that need to be adjusted for the new role.

One of the most enriching experiences we get to see a couple of times a year is watching a young leader working through our ***Building New & Maturing Leader*** management training program get the "oh wow" impact when they see the light regarding what their role really entails. Sometime it comes during one of the training sessions, other times during one of their individual coaching sessions. In all cases, they see the role with more clarity and how they can do even minor things just a little differently to get different results.

It's this break point you are searching for regarding your own behaviors as a leader. Do one thing a day in your new role wearing that special

26

new role hat. Persevere day after day; seek the clearing of the fog, and smile as you achieve your own "oh wow" experience.

## Coaching Thoughts – For You and Your Peers

- What are some of the things you know you need to do, but feel that you don't have the time or resources for? How can you break these down according to this "do one thing each day" philosophy?

- Re-read the first paragraph. Why do you think the phrases "management stuff" and "real work" are set apart by quotation marks? Is the "real work" more important than the "management stuff"? Or are the tasks of a manager just as valid as the work done by their employees?

# A Trip Through the Valley of Despair

Change is happening all the time. Modern theory on change tells us we will work through a fairly typical pattern of denial, despair, acceptance and then hopefully engagement with moving forward. But it's our visitation to the valley of despair segment that can cause the most consternation, and how long someone stays in the valley of despair definitely impacts the intensity of their future engagement.

Think of the change as traveling from one mountain top to another separated by a valley. Your employees are standing together on the first mountain top looking towards the next mountain – the destination – but each of the employees sees the valley much differently.

- A short hike down the grassy hill to the meadow in the valley.

- A deep valley with a small river to cross.

- An immense cliff with a class 5 rapid running through the distant valley below.

And there you are. . . almost summiting the new mountain yelling back to your team not to worry about the short climb as you gain energy and excitement with your healthy engagement of the new destination.

Is the rate at which a person can work through "change" directly proportional to the maturity of their leader? Not entirely. But great, mature leaders have learned to always carry some strong rope, know how to teach the art of rappelling down cliffs, and understand that talking is much easier when you're next to someone.

**Coaching Thoughts – For You and Your Peers**

- There is a lot of metaphor in this Leadership Learning Moment. Look back at the three views of the valley described in the bullet points and try to work out what each one means in terms of change in the workplace.

- What about the phrase, "…great, mature leaders have learned to always carry some strong rope, know how to teach the art of rappelling down cliffs, and understand that talking is much easier when you're next to someone"? What does this mean to a leader guiding his team through change?

# Back to the Line. Do It Again.

Sometimes you have to go back to square one of your management training and practice the basics.

Sports coaches know well that players must keep their basic skills fully in tune. Pro football coaches bring their guys back to the line again and again during practices to run the same play. College soccer coaches run their players through foot skills over and over. They know that building the instinctual behaviors for excellent play requires repetition to build the muscle memory. They practice like they play.

In your big, bad leadership role, how often are you coming back to the line to practice the basics of supervision and management?

Experience shows us that just going through the motions of management is terribly transparent to those that matter most. And the more elevated your role in the organization the more significant the impact from the gap between real management and going through the motions.

**Coaching Thoughts – For You and Your Peers**

- What do you do to keep your management skills in shape? Are you practicing like you play?

- Think of a time when your "muscle memory" of leadership skills failed you. What did you do to resolve the issue? Do you think you could have avoided the issue if you'd had more practice with the basics of supervision and management?

# Traversing the Ditch

The Fiscal Cliff mantra of late 2012 brought tremendous, terrifying images to mind for many people. Who wants to go over a cliff? A good friend of mine adjusted the lens looking at the forthcoming events as a Fiscal Ditch which was quite refreshing. We can traverse a ditch.

Challenges lay ahead for you and your team. As the well-informed, dynamic leader you, of course, can foresee the depth and breadth of these challenges. The choice you need to make is how best to communicate the information you have, to elicit the motivation and behaviors you desire of your team.

The truth is always your friend. Be choosy with the words you leverage in describing the truth.

**Coaching Thoughts – For You and Your Peers**

- Think of a time when you had to communicate some difficult information to your team.

    o   How did you do it?

    o   What would you do differently if you could go back?

- What do you think is meant by the caution at the end of this Leadership Learning Moment: "Be choosy with the words you leverage in describing the truth."?

31

# Being Timely, Specific, and Sincere

One of the easiest and most impactful kinds of feedback to give is positive feedback. It motivates and builds commitment, and do people really ever get tired of hearing they've done a good job?

The first step – and this is crucial – is to notice what's gone well. Next, follow these simple rules.

- **Make it timely** - as soon as you see it, don't delay

- **Make it specific** - go beyond saying "good job" – what did you like about what you saw? How did it help? What made it "good?"

- **Make it sincere** - mean what you say and comment on something that is important and will make a difference.

With the right relationship and right recognition, people will want to put forth more effort for you and you'll be tapping into a person's discretionary energy – that optional extra effort a person can put forth every day and decide whether or not they are going to.

Remember: People will repeat the positive behaviors you notice.

**Coaching Thoughts – For You and Your Peers**

- This Leadership Learning Moment is discussing positive feedback, but could you apply the same guidelines to constructive feedback as well? Or would you need to modify it?

- Have you ever noticed something going well and neglected to mention it? Or has this ever happened to you? How did it affect your employee's (or your) discretionary energy?

# The Fallacy of "I'm A Working Manager"

"I'm a working manager. I just don't have the time to do all these management things I'm supposed to do"

Yes, you are a working manager. And so is every other person out there who is responsible for leading and managing other people. Every foreman, supervisor, team leader, manager, senior manager, project manager, assistant director, director, VP, Senior VP, Executive VP, Super Secret Very Special Senior VP, CIO, COO, CFO, CAO, CCO, CTO, CHRO, CVO, CMO, GM, CEO, Divisional CEO, Chairman.

You can choose to use the "but I'm a working manager" phrase as an excuse to make yourself feel better. But truth is your friend, and the truth is. . . .

- Managing people *is* work.

- You have a lot of things – tasks, projects, meetings, work – to get done.

- You have needy employees who are not fully trained, never will be, and who don't have the same ambition and drive you perceive yourself to have or had when you were just an employee.

- You are accountable and responsible for the workload and mistakes of your employees.

- You are an adult, living in a free country and had the option to take the role you've chosen.

Now that we have that settled, what's your next move? You can wallow in the vast black hole of "woe is me", falsely comforting yourself in comparisons of how hard you work compared to Joe over there while you ignore your responsibility. Or you can woman up/man up, thank God for the opportunity you have to be employed making more money than 95% of the people in this world, and take seriously the responsibility that you have signed up for: that is, to manage and lead people.

Managing people is work. If it's too much trouble then you should consider walking over to HR to announce your decision to be demoted to an individual contributor with a full salary reduction to the average wage for employees in that role.

**Coaching Thoughts – For You and Your Peers**

- Have you ever caught yourself thinking of your leadership duties as "not real work"?

- What happens to the employees under you if you don't give your work as a manager the proper attention or training?

# Re-Assessing Your Planning Assumptions

Are you struggling as a leader to figure out how you'll get everything done? Consider adjusting your "planning assumptions": those parameters or guidelines that act as guard rails to keep you aligned on your original path. Planning assumptions are great when they help to keep you moving forward on autopilot, creating managerial habits. But sometimes we take these planning assumptions for granted, not realizing how they may limit our perspective or block potential opportunities.

Great leaders seize upon opportunities to take a timeout to identify, challenge, and adjust their planning assumptions periodically. Intellectually, this sounds simple enough. But the real work comes in identifying your planning assumptions because often, these are deeply ingrained in your habits and culture.

**Coaching Thoughts – For You and Your Peers**

- Invest 30 minutes to thinking to honestly and identify your planning assumptions, then challenge yourself to address those areas which are either too enabling or too restrictive. Write down your prime directive and think: how does it drive your decision making?

- How you have created work structures around the needs of your employees? How would your replacement deal with the special work arrangements you've made with your employees?

  o Would the new boss allow Johnny to continue working a staggered schedule?

  o Would he/she dismantle your work flow and processes?

- o   Would he/she limit the specialization of work or internal partnerships?

- What about your prime directive (that overriding theme driving your vision for where your team or organization is heading): would the new boss agree with that?

# The Three Misuses of Spotlight by Managers

Are you using a spotlight or a floodlight when you review an employee's performance? A spotlight is directed, tight, and narrow in its focus, able to illuminate specific targets, like an actor on a stage. A floodlight is broad, less discriminating, and wide in dispersing light to see more of what's actually going on.

Spotlights can be very effective in the right environments, but are terribly ineffective when used in the wrong places.

- **Highlighting the One** – A spotlight shined upon a single singer during a duet performance leaves someone in the dark. Though we can hear the music, we give all of our attention to that one person. When manager focuses on the success of one employee alone, he may be missing the role others played in that success.

- **Too Lazy to Change the Light** – Quickly moving a spotlight across a stage to try to catch all the actors may show each actor for a second, but it wastes a lot of energy and time. Changing to a floodlight will illuminate more space at any given time, allowing for more to be seen by providing appropriate illumination to all participants. As a manager, running from meeting to meeting and email to email, are you rushing around with a spotlight focus? Or are you taking a moment to soak in the full view of a situation, conversation, or email? Change the light and broaden your view to see all that's going on and to make good, informed decisions.

- **Time to Fire** – Looking at the performance of an employee over 12 months with a spotlight perspective will give you keen

38

insight to specific points in time, revealing specific behaviors and results. This is fully appropriate when you are seeking examples to illuminate your feedback. But when the spotlight is used to only pick out the examples of bad behavior in order to substantiate a rash decision on firing an employee, you are likely to miss circumstantial evidence of how you and others may have played a role in the poor performance.

Your focus and perspective are biased from the get go, but you can choose to adjust the lighting to help you gain perspective. In the end, you will think your decisions are right whether you adjust or not. But what will your employees or peers or bosses or customers believe? To lead well, a manager must make new choices and adapt new behaviors to increase their capacity to lead.

## Coaching Thoughts – For You and Your Peers

- Think of a time when adjusting your perspective (going from a spotlight to a floodlight) influenced a decision you made. How might it have turned out if you hadn't done so?

- Why do you think it is so important for leaders to be able to make new choices and adapt new behaviors?

- This Leadership Learning Moment describes the positives of using a broad floodlight to illuminate perspective. But are there some situations when a spotlight focus could be a good thing? If so, what might some of those be?

# Cultivating the True Grit of Your Employees

Why is it that some employees are just heads and tails above others? It's not that they are the most talented in the bunch, though they do have some talent. And it's not that they work the hardest all the time, though they do work hard. Rather, it is more that they work hard every day with persistence towards the long term goal that has been established, persevering through obstacles to keep moving the ball forward. They have a tenacity- or zeal, or passion- for the work at hand.

Psychologists who have studied this particular attribute have labeled it "grit" (take a look at Angela Lee Duckworth's TED video for more on the topic). Grit is the desire that drives a person toward goals, ends, or objectives when others would just give up and go home. Grit is the reason that tenacious, above-average athletes can make it through Navy Seal training while the most talented national athletes simply give up. Individuals with grit have a positive, optimistic perspective of the long term: they are more focused on winning the marathon than the sprint.

There's an expectation of you as a leader to be able to build and focus on the long term goals while motivating others towards these goals. The Wright brothers were able to do this. Abraham Lincoln was able to do this. And thousands of no-name managers, supervisors, foremen, VPs, and CEOs have been able to do this. These leaders weren't the most talented people out there, they didn't have the perfect pedigrees for leadership, and they didn't take a magic pill to become gritty leaders. They were already gritty.

The same can be said about some of your employees: they are already gritty. The deep question you should be asking yourself is this: how do I enable and cultivate the grit that each employee already has?

1. Start by getting you own Grit Score. Go to www.sas.upenn.edu/~duckwort/ and scroll down to the bottom and locate the Get Your Grit Score link in the table.

2. Watch the TED video.

3. Create a scoring for how you see your employees' grit level.

4. Think hard about 3 or 4 employees and how you could better enable their work environment to cultivate their grittiness.

Finally, add this book to your summer reading list and awaken those biased perceptions which may be hindering your people decisions: *Talent Is Overrated: What Really Separates World-Class Performers from Everybody Else* by Geoff Colvin.

## Coaching Thoughts – For You and Your Peers

- Take a moment to think about, then answer the question posed at the end of this Leadership Learning Moment: "How do I enable and cultivate the grit that each employee already has?"

- What about yourself? What are some ways that you can enable and cultivate your own grit?

# Wearing Multiple Hats

In a recent discussion with a CEO regarding her career path up through the finance function of an organization, it was revealed that she still maintained full functional responsibility for finance and accounting since she had chosen to not replace herself as CFO. Nor had she replaced her prior role of Controller.

It's intriguing to think about how she handles the multi-level role she fulfills as the boss while also performing a peer functional role with some of her direct reports. For instance, when is the Controller hat replaced with the CEO hat in discussions regarding spending cuts across an organization?

**Coaching Thoughts – For You and Your Peers**

- We all have tasks, projects, teams, business functions, divisions, subsidiary companies which are near and dear to our hearts for emotional or comfort reasons. But when do these anomalies limit our ability to be fully enabled for our primary role?

- What unintended behavioral ripples might we be initiating in the organization's culture?

# Twitterize Performance Feedback

The art of delivering relevant performance feedback hinges upon your ability as a manager to recognize a teachable/coachable moment, capture a mental video clip of the behavior exhibited and then create and deliver the insight. These skills aren't natural for most managers and therefore need to be built and refined over time.

**Practice like you play.** Build up and practice your feedback delivery skills every day to create the mental muscles and courage needed to maximize teachable moments. Twitter's 140 character restriction provides a great practice platform for developing/enhancing your capability to deliver concise feedback. Thinking in Twitteresque 140 characters or less sounds bites will force you to focus upon the key behavior you'd liked repeated or eliminated. Here are two examples.

*Max, I liked your manufacturing update this morning; your format of 2 positives/2 challenges helped us visualize the situation.*

*Max, your manufacturing update this morning was a bit long/confusing: is it possible for you to deliver just the key items in half the time?*

Just to be clear, I'm not suggesting that you actually post your feedback on Twitter via employee hashtags. Either draft the updates in Twitter or simply use features in Word, or your favorite tool, to count the number of characters in your draft.

**Coaching Thoughts – For You and Your Peers**

- Have you ever had a boss give you feedback in a way that stuck in your memory (either for a good or bad reason)? How might this advice have affected that situation?

- How does this "Twitter strategy" make it easier to take advantage of teachable moments?

# Blah, Blah, Blah... Reorg Coming... Blah, Blah, Blah

From a recent CEO: "We have a lot to do. The most pressing thing I heard from our town hall meetings was the desire to clearly define our vision and strategy. I promise you we will be transparent and plan to articulate this in the coming weeks."

What employees hear: "Blah, blah, blah . . .more work . . . blah, blah, blah . . . reorg coming . . . blah blah, blah . . . co-workers are going to lose their jobs . . . blah, blah, blah . . . some exec is getting a big bonus . . ."

When you start talking as if you are the focal point in a Dilbert cartoon, it might be time to look behind you and see who exactly has followed you over the hill.

### Coaching Thoughts – For You and Your Peers

- How can you talk to your employees about potential changes, etc. *without* sounding like the focal point of a Dilbert cartoon? Try to come up with some concrete ideas.

- What are some ways that communication between leaders and employees falls short in your organization? What steps could you take to begin to improve this?

#Leadwell

# Gaining Perspective

#Leadwell

# Adjust Your Paradigm: Fire Yourself

We all can get caught up in our self-perception regarding how important we are in our leadership roles, as well as the effectiveness we enable within our organization as fairly decent leaders. Leadership effectiveness is dependent upon your capability to leverage relationships to achieve goals. The depth and breadth of these professional relationships depend heavily on the level of activity you invest in them.

I find many executives limit their investment in building and sustaining the quality of professional relationships within their current organization and, as importantly, outside their organization. They are with colleagues in meetings all the time, but there is little investment in building the quality of those relationships.

Take 15 minutes to fire yourself and review your relationships.

- Quickly, handwrite a 2 sentence memo firing yourself.

- Make a list of the 20 people you would contact to let them know about your transition.

- Make note of when was the last time you had real contact with each of these 20 people, with contact defined as meeting for lunch, dinner, coffee or a phone conversation.

- Make a list of who within your current organization could – and would – provide a recommendation on your leadership capability.

- Assess your LinkedIn profile. How many contacts do you maintain? How up-to-date is your profile?

The paradigm exploration you should seek is to inventory your relationships, taking note of whom you should be investing time with to make sure you're in tune with their professional and personal lives. It's likely that the converse will be true and they will be in tune with your life. Now, imagine if you had their real time perspective/advice/input on your leadership challenges.

**Coaching Thoughts – For You and Your Peers**

- Ask yourself: Am I willing to commit to meet with one person a week over the next 20 weeks to increase the depth and breadth of my relationships and gain perspective on the growth of my leadership capability?

- Take the 15 minutes to fire yourself, using the steps outlined above. What is the result?

# Thomas Jefferson's Trend Line

Reading well-written biographies provides a great opportunity to place myself in the life and times of the focus of the book. Recently I read Jon Meacham's Thomas Jefferson: The Art of Power, a tremendous, deep dive into Jefferson's use of all his talents. Jefferson was exceptional at knowing how to distill complexity into a comprehensible message to reach the minds as well as the hearts of the larger world.

Here are three leadership learning moments from Jefferson's life.

**The Art of Soft Power** – Jefferson was not directly confrontational. He leveraged his broad knowledge, deep intellect, extreme curiosity, and engaging personality to open and maintain conversations with all people, allowing him the opportunity to gain tremendous insight. Understanding people and their potential/likely reactions to complex scenarios allows leaders to guide decisions and influence outcomes.

**Know Your Prime Directives** – Staying the course with your vision over extended periods of time with unwavering force can be difficult. Jefferson lived and led through the formation and launching of our nation. Nothing was guaranteed, and forces of politics and nature were constantly creating headwinds. Jefferson maintained his focus on the opportunity our country had with deploying and growing democracy while inciting individual liberty. He intently focused decision-making on what would enable the long term success of the union and transcend the experiment of democracy to become the bedrock of democracy. Great leaders see the big picture and stay the course.

**Lead Well When Called Upon** – At the ripe age of 33, Jefferson was asked to compose the draft for our Declaration of Independence. Under the threat of treason and the contentious editing and verbal debate from young, rebellious, nation-forming leaders, he enabled the completion of a transformative document that sparked the birth of our country. Great leaders step up and play the roles they need to play to enable transformation.

Jefferson wasn't perfect, and he did have many flaws. But the trend line of his leadership through decades was positive and is still impactful today. Recognize that you aren't perfect but that you are living in great times, and determine today how you will lead well to improve your trend line.

**Coaching Thoughts – For You and Your Peers**

- What are some actionable steps you could take to improve your trend line according to the leadership learning moments from Jefferson's life?

- When was the last time you read an inspiring biography? Choose one, then try to find at least three "leadership learning moments" from the subject's life that you can apply to your own.

# Are You Using the Information Pipeline for Good or Evil?

Part of the art of leadership is the give and take of that information which is not common knowledge. There's a barter of sorts which occurs between leaders as they share bits and pieces of information they know, or sort of know, or are conjuring up as they piece together disparate information. Some folks seem to have a lot of information to share; others, not so much.

Within every organization, there is an informal pipeline of information that goes among and between leaders and employees. Leaders add their bits and pieces of information to this flow, and as they do, they either increase or decrease the current – the speed – of the information flow.

The quality of the information flow is always subject. We all know that as information is passed around again and again, the quality tends to decrease, become soiled, and sometimes even be totally destroyed. The information is massaged and interpreted in a multitude of ways, sometimes for the better and sometimes for the worse.

The size of the pipeline may conversely correlate to the capability of top leadership to communicate well, meaning the less the executives are talking the more likely employees will make up wild and crazy stories. But this isn't always the case, as some great organizations encourage a large informal communication pipeline because the pipeline creates agility and connects both sources and consumers of key information more efficiently.

**Coaching Thoughts – For You and Your Peers**

- Whether your organization uses the information this way or not, take a moment to think about your last 10 informal discussions with peers or employees.

  o What information was shared in that conversation?

  o Since you were the source of input to the information pipeline, so to speak, what were your intentions with the sharing and what was the quality of the information being discussed?

    ▪ Did you increase the clarity of the flow, or only make it murkier?

    ▪ Did you help make the organization more productive?

- As you ponder these questions, remember: the higher up you are in the food chain is directly proportional to the impact and speed you will have on the information and pipeline. Make wise decisions regarding the what, how, when and why of your addition to the flow.

# Three Fears You Should Have When Considering a Promotion

A promotion brings tremendous thrill and excitement. But seasoned leaders realize that those feelings are short-lived. Their hard-won wisdom tells them a promotion's short honeymoon will be followed by three times as much work as they had before. As you get promoted, especially to your first management position, you should anticipate these fears:

1. **The Fear of New Boss** — The opportunity to start fresh with a new boss who has all your interests in mind is so compelling. You feel supported and believed in, and you likely are. But beware of the momentary sigh or pause where you can see a change in energy. This is the transition your boss makes as he decide the honeymoon is over and now it's time to get you trained to work the way he needs you to work. The bit is going in the mouth, and the reins will start to be pulled.

2. **The Fear of "That" Project** — With a new role comes some new projects which you will be responsible for leading. Most of the projects will indeed be challenging and stimulating, but beware of "that" project; the one that's been percolating since your predecessor left. The project with unrealistic dates, an ever-increasing scope of work, and tired resources... and likely a pet project of your new boss.

3. **The Fear of Buyer's Remorse** — Usually it comes towards the end of the 2nd day in the new role. That sinking, horrible feeling of "what have I gotten myself into and why didn't I listen to my wife/friend/mentor/co-worker?". You've made a LinkedIn profile-building, career advancement decision, there's

no good way to retreat, and besides, the money is good. But the job is a bad reality TV show waiting to happen.

Think long and hard about that promotion opportunity before you say yes. Don't be enticed by the lure of how great it will be, because in the end it will likely be a tougher job than you imagine, and the money might not cover the pain and agony. You will need a deeper well of fortitude to draw from, which comes from following your passion and/or going into the role with eyes wide open.

## Coaching Thoughts – For You and Your Peers

- When facing a new promotion, what are some things you might do to go into the role "with eyes wide open"?

- Are the three fears articulated here meant to serve as a stop or a yield sign? In other words, should you automatically say no to a promotion if it is going to actualize one of these fears, or should you just proceed with caution?

- Can you think of any additional advice you might give someone considering a promotion opportunity?

# Lessons from Lawn Mower Racing

Each summer our neighborhood in upstate NY comes together for the *Rick Braiman Memorial Lawn Mower Race*. A race course is designed new each year to weave among several homes and around obstacles, requiring racers to negotiate chaos-inducing spots. Our recent race included two laps with two drivers, creating a "difficult" change of drivers event.

The race provides us with an opportunity to come together as a broad family, bonding over pre- and post-race stories and remembering our friend and neighbor Rick. He passed away in 2003 from pancreatic cancer, and the culture of our neighborhood was forever changed by Rick's passing. It left a scar that is always present, despite the healing work of time.

Five lessons I've learned from lawn mower racing:

1. While racing a lawn mower is something of an oxymoron given the speed we actually travel, we can feel like we are flying around the course if we set our expectations appropriately. How might your employees – or you – feel with well-established expectations?

2. A race reveals a winner only when they are surrounded by their competition. If you win and you're all alone, have you really won anything? Your team's success comes on the shoulders of teams who have come before you.

3. Traditional events, while often goofy, have tremendous meaning. The kids in our neighborhood who have grown up watching the race each year actually see more than just the event itself: they see a life lived together as a broad family.

57

What traditions have you created, enabled or supported with your team or company?

4.  Folding in new neighbors to our historic race creates an opportunity to feed them with the rich history of our neighborhood culture... but we must first invite them to the race. As new employees come to your team, make sure to invite them into the culture and whatever goofy events make your team who they are.

5.  Honoring the memory of a lost friend helps to heal the scar that will always be present, and helps us to keep perspective on the fragility of our relationships and life. Make sure to honor well those who reveal the essence of your culture with clear delineation from those who don't.

Leading well requires us to see the forest for the trees, to take the time and invest the energy to make the right things happen. Are you investing well?

**Coaching Thoughts – For You and Your Peers**

-   Think about some of the traditions you have (whether they are with family, friends, or peers at work). Pick one and make your own list: "Top Five Things I've Learned from Our _____ Tradition".

-   How can you apply these life lessons to other areas of your life?

-   Try to come up with several actionable steps you could take.

-   Lesson #5 in this Leadership Learning Moment says to "honor well those who reveal the essence of your culture, with clear delineation from those who don't"? Why do you think this is so important to leadership?

- Take a moment to think about your team's strengths and identify the weaknesses. Could starting a goofy tradition of your own help your team to improve in this area?

# Failing at Leading Above Your Ability NFL Replacement Referees

Luckily for most maturing leaders, there aren't cameras rolling and a national audience of 16 million people watching as they make critical mistakes. The NFL "replacement referees" have been trained in their craft but have been working as referees in less intense, less demanding levels than the NFL. It would seem that these replacements would be fine but as this now infamous picture reveals from the last play of September 24, 2012 Monday Night Football Game, performing well at a higher level demands a lot.

Maturing leaders gain ground every month as they experience more situations testing out their skills. Ideally these leaders are building wisdom that can be brought to bear in future situations. Unfortunately, organizations aren't usually patient enough to allow these maturing leaders to ripen or season well over time; the leaders are thrown into larger and more complex roles way too early.

There are many employees at all levels who see so much wrong with these bosses and their behaviors and lack of leadership capability. What's so interesting is to listen to group of mid-level managers who see all that is wrong with the senior leaders while having no clue or insight to how unhappy and disgruntled their own employees are with their bosses.

We could place all leaders on Reality TV so the audience could see, decipher, criticize leaders' behaviors and leverage online voting to filter out those who stink from those who perform well. Or we could create an apprentice program that helps leaders to build upon their craft with support and guidance and corrective action as necessary. Or we could just continue to throw untrained, half-effective leaders into much larger and more complex roles hoping for the best outcomes because we're sure they will just figure it out along the way.

**Coaching Thoughts – For You and Your Peers**

- The NFL Replacement Refs have now been demoted as the real referees come back on the scene. When was the last time you heard of a less-than-effective leader in your organization being demoted <u>and</u> their pay adjusted to reflect their position change?

- Does your organization or team offer adequate training for those promoted to a new role? Or are they left with shoes that are too big to fill?

# Collisions to Tease Your Brain

What happens when you read *Team of Rivals: The Political Genius of Abraham Lincoln*, a book about President Lincoln's leadership of his purposefully diverse cabinet, followed by C.S. Lewis' *Mere Christianity*, a transcription of radio shows communicating the common and basics beliefs of Christianity? Collisions in the mind that stretch the boundaries of common thought and (hopefully) make your head hurt a bit.

Leaders get stuck in ruts of how to behave and end up as only "somewhat effective". They work in discrete business functions most often encompassing the fields in which their careers began. So the CIO was once a programmer, the CFO was once an accounts payable clerk, the VP of HR was once a recruiter, and so on. This insulated, functional career approach limits the availability of collisions of the mind as these leaders question less and less of what can and can't be accomplished within the business function. Unfortunately, they come to think they are good leaders when, in fact, they are just adequate managers who have a depth of functional knowledge and big, bad job titles.

Great leaders develop creative thinking skills and leverage a curiosity of how things could be, how individual talent could be developed, what teams could accomplish. They tease their brains to think in abnormal ways. They read books and articles from extremely disparate sources. They seek out assignments and roles in a variety of business functions and companies where they can test their leadership mettle. The resulting collisions of thought, experience, and wisdom create a unique leadership competency.

Challenge yourself to be a better leader by seeking collisions in your personal development. Start by reading disparate books in succession and letting your mind ponder the collisions of thought. Tease your brain to think in abnormal – healthy abnormal – ways.

**Coaching Thoughts – For You and Your Peers**

- In the second-to-last paragraph, this Leadership Learning Moment gives several examples of how you can stretch your mind as a leader. Are there other ways (in other areas of your life) that you can create collisions of thought to help you grow? Try to think outside of the box.

- Do you think stretching your boundaries outside of work (like taking a dance class with your spouse, or volunteering regularly at a food pantry) would benefit you as a leader? If so, how?

- Make a bucket list of things you're going to do to create collisions of thought in your life. Include things both at work and outside of work… and stick to it.

- Do you know a leader who seems stuck in the rut of his (or her) too-big title of manager? How can you encourage them to grow?

# Marissa Mayer's Radical Leadership

Uproar, controversy, and disbelief. The business world and thousands of bloggers wonder how golden girl Marissa Mayer, CEO of Yahoo, could make such a horrible decision regarding remote employees. How could this high-tech executive—the 20th employee at Google, the builder of the successful teams that launched Gmail, Google Maps, and iGoogle, and the woman recruited to be the savior of Yahoo—make such a decision?

Well, it's fairly simple: she is a radical leader leading courageously.

Leaders should . . .

1. **See the Landscape** – Great leaders go to the tops of the trees and look out over the forest to the horizon to see what terrain the company must navigate and how the environmental factors may impact the path forward. We couldn't foresee what Steve Jobs saw with the value of the iPhone; nor can we foresee what Marissa Mayer sees as she scans the horizon.

2. **Lead the Team** – Great leaders transform teams to excel at plotting courses of action and making good (and sometimes extremely tough) decisions. While the media focuses on tarnishing a high profile CEO, I'm more curious about Yahoo's executive team and their moment of truth as they either pull together in support of "their" decision or cower in the corner. Mayer is appropriately taking on her role and leading forward; time will reveal how well she builds teams.

3. **Keep the Body Alive** – Companies fail. Yahoo was failing. Great doctors know drastic measures are needed at times to save a life. Radical, invasive treatments bring human bodies near death in order to be saved. Great leaders must have the vision

and guts to take failing companies through radical treatments in order to save their organization.

14,000-plus employees trust their livelihood and future on the ability of Marissa Mayer and the Yahoo executive team to lead the company forward. They are paid an extreme amount of money to make tough decisions and lead the company through the valley of despair to survival. While on the surface it appears that Yahoo's policy change is destructive, we really have no idea how this decision fits within the fabric of decisions Mayer and her executive team are weaving. But we do know this: leaders must make hard decisions.

**Coaching Thoughts – For You and Your Peers**

- When was the last time you faced a touch leadership decision? How did you lead your team radically and courageously? If you had read the three guidelines listed in this Leadership Learning Moment, would you have done anything differently?

- Imagine that your team is struggling in some way. Take a moment to walk through each of these steps, coming up with concrete actions you could take for each one to help your team survive.

- How would you "See the Landscape"? "Lead the Team"? What would you do to "Keep the Body Alive"?

# Pray for Me: The Silencing of 100,000 Onlookers

Historically analyzing transformational change allows us to see the moments in time when leaders have articulated profoundly simple visions, and the resulting behavioral change that occurred over time within an organization or group after the proclamation. JFK's "landing a man on the moon and returning him safely to earth" speech is one example. Paul O'Neil's opening vision statement as he took over Alcoa ("I intend to make Alcoa the safest company in America. I intend to go for zero injuries") is another. The resulting tectonic shifts in long-term behavior and success were profound, though difficult to see day-to-day during the transformations.

This week we have witnessed such a profound, vision-shifting proclamation. With just a few authentic words and slight yet discerning shifts in traditional behavior, the newly-elected Pope Francis spoke volumes to the worldwide organization of 412,000 priests and 1.2 billion followers he now leads. He conveyed the shift in approach he expects, showed his priorities, and spoke clearly to the essence of the purpose he foresees.

Many books and articles have been written about servant leadership. Pope Francis is a living example of a servant leader leading a serving organization. And his authentic leadership is revealed in the alignment of what he thinks, what he says, and what he does.

**Coaching Thoughts – For You and Your Peers**

- How will *you* stand up today as an authentic leader?

- What do you think about the term "servant leadership"? Is that something that only works in a serving organization? Or could you apply it to you position in your organization as well?

# Embrace the Struggle

When we struggle as managers, we often feel inadequate. We may wonder quietly why we took the job in the first place, but we definitely do not want to talk with others about our struggles. But times of great strain create defining moments in who we are and how we can lead. The struggle itself is the trigger that we can use to tell our reflective brains to listen up and learn something, especially after the fact while we are reflecting upon the events.

In *Leadership and the Art of Struggle*, Steven Snyder speaks to the tension that all great struggles bring. Tension is a byproduct of change, and it forces managers to be off-balance. While tension can come from various sources – tradition, relationships, aspirations, and identity – it's the automatic responses we develop to these tension points that can cause confusion. Self-exploration of these tension areas could provide insight as to why we are confused. And telling others our stories could provide them with wisdom and insight.

Unfortunately, mangers at all levels are fearful of telling their "struggle stories" for fear of showing their weaknesses and failures. Ironically, it is in the telling of these stories that great insight can be found, not only for the storyteller but also for those listening.

**Coaching Thoughts – For You and Your Peers**

- Think about some of the most defining moments in your career as a leader. Was there struggle for you? Great stress and difficulty? Was the defining moment character-building?

- Take time to catalog a few stories of struggles you've encountered as a leader. At the right moments, you can tell a story to your peers or your boss and encourage them to tell you

68

their stories.  You may be surprised at what wisdom you'll pick up along the way.

# The Rippling Impact of Dishonorable, Narcissistic Leadership

When an employee makes a dishonorable decision, they create small ripples of hurt. When executives make dishonorable decisions, they hurt whole organizations of people as well as those with whom the people interact. Hundreds if not thousands of people are impacted.

There's a standard to which most of us hold ourselves: a moral compass, a value system, a belief in doing the right thing. But every now and then, we come across an executive whose selfish, narcissistic, inappropriate behavior creates a terrible and long-lasting ripple of distrust, heartbreak, and disappointment. The wave of impact ripples through the organization person by person and team by team, and though the wave decreases in intensity as it bounces around, there's a longevity to it as the ripples keep rolling outward.

- **Employees' trust barometers go haywire.** They wonder which other executives are doing bad things. All executives and managers are lumped together into a perceived pool of powerful people who—when prompted with self-interest or greed or entitlement—will make selfish choices. None are to be fully trusted.

- **Young managers lose their bearings.** These impressionable leaders looking for role models to reveal the art and science of good management and leadership wonder just who they should emulate. They find themselves the object of collateral scorn while grieving the tarnish to their profession and unrewarded daily effort to do the right things.

- **Families and communities lose momentum.** Every employee goes home and seeks some level of support from their families, friends, and those within their communities with whom they interact. With each conversation, the burden is spread and the impact ripples further. Conversations trend negative. Disappointment abounds. Another thin layer of belief in people with power taking proper care of the precious resources is sanded away.

It is so disappointing that the few who make such poor decisions have such a large impact on the rest of us.

Kudos to those leaders who remain in the organization to carry the burden; to those leaders who get up every day to strive to lead well in the face of adversity; to those leaders who will invest heavily to re-build trust. And kudos to those leaders who will ignore legal counsel advice in order to tell future companies seeking references on these dishonored leaders that they shouldn't hire them.

**Coaching Thoughts – For You and Your Peers**

- Have you ever been affected by someone's dishonorable, narcissistic leadership? What happened? What did you do to minimize the damage? What could you have done differently?

- Take a moment to clarify what the moral standard that you hold yourself to is, then write it down clearly and articulately. Use it as a reference when making decisions to prevent yourself from becoming an accidental dishonorable, narcissistic leader.

# Baltimore Ravens: A Great Parallel Team

My favorite NFL football team, the Baltimore Ravens, will play in the Super Bowl this Sunday. The team is catching the perfect wave at exactly the right point in time. The head coach, the coaching staff, the influential leaders, and all the players are positioned to follow their playbooks and leverage their building momentum to victory. The Ravens have built the best *parallel team* for this season.

The great Peter Drucker provided us with a perspective on varying types of teams – fixed position, parallel, and innovative – and which environments enable the best team structures. A football team, like an orchestra, must synthesize the performance of sub teams to come together to accomplish the goal at hand and, as such, are parallel teams. The better the sub teams perform in conjunction with each other the better the final product.

Parallel teams are more flexible allowing players working simultaneously to cover for one another more easily. The playbook, or musical score, provides the exact specifications required to be successful while each player is expected to perform at the highest level. The leaders will direct the play calls and guide the team. At specific moments in time, some players will be asked to perform a solo revealing their individual creativeness and exceptional ability.

John Harbaugh, head coach for the Ravens, didn't just decide last week that the team should come together: he led them here.

- He invested time building relationships since the summer as well as over the years.

- He encouraged player growth and development.

- He synchronized the egos of leaders and facilitated crucial conversations.

- He made the hard decisions, for instance firing his 2nd in command, offensive coordinator Cam Cameron, at a critical point late in the season.

- He believed and guided a culture of belief.

Will all this be enough to win on Sunday? Probably. Because great teams catching perfect waves don't just stand there waiting for the glory. Great teams pull together to create the opportunity for glory to be revealed.

### Go Ravens!!

### Coaching Thoughts – For You and Your Peers

- Take a moment to reflect on the bullet points in this leadership learning moment. Which ones come easily to your team? Which might you need to work on to transform from an okay team to a great parallel team?

- What do you think about this statement: "A team, like an orchestra, must synthesize the performance of sub teams to come together to accomplish the goal at hand." Does this ring true to you? What can you do within your own team to reflect this?

#Leadwell

# Creating Habits

#Leadwell

# Be a Weird Manager

Normal managers are everywhere: in fact, most managers are virtually the same in the way they manage and lead their teams. These normal managers follow the status quo of the culture and fight to maintain the mediocrity of entitled management, wearing their self-proclaimed status symbols of "Back to Back Meetings" and "250 Emails a Day" as badges of honor. Normal managers enjoy their entitled position but still feel underpaid for what they bring to the business. Normal managers will only meet with employees when they are told to by Human Resources at performance review time. Normal managers work hard to fit in among their peers and bosses, seeking to increase their status within the organization.

Great managers are actually weird managers. The way they manage is so different that they don't fit the cultural mold. They seem a little off-beat and not in sync with the other managers. They are constantly talking with employees about their work, giving feedback at every opportune moment. Weird managers prefer to run meetings that are no longer than 19 minutes. Weird managers take a full lunch, seeking rejuvenation and collegial exposure. Weird managers seize found time as opportunities for investment in others. Weird managers know the names of their employees... and the names of those employees' spouses/significant others, their kids, and their hobbies. Weird managers seem to know exactly when they need to inject some motivational juice into an employee. Weird managers go off script during "transitional conversations", and are the first to provide LinkedIn connections to displaced employees.

Where do you fall on the list of Normal Managers versus Weird Managers?

- Normal Managers inhale their lunch in 12 minutes, sitting by themselves at their desk while reading emails and checking the weather. Weird Managers take a full hour for lunch, leaving the building to go to a favorite spot to rejuvenate over a leisurely lunch. Often, they eat with someone else whose company they enjoy.

- Normal Managers complain when their spot bonus rewards budget is cut. Weird managers take money from their own pocket to reward employees and their teams for great work.

- Normal managers feel unproductive when some of their back-to-back meetings are cancelled for the day. Weird Managers invest cancelled meeting time with walking and talking among their employees.

- Normal Managers dread performance review time. Weird Managers provide performance reviews every day.

- Normal Managers sit on the deck of their vacation home, sipping cocktails and telling stories about the difficult reorganization they led their department/business function/company through. Weird Managers sit at the table on their vacation home deck writing anonymous $3,000 checks from their personal accounts to each displaced employee, hoping that the funds will somehow help them through the difficult times.

You are paid a more than fair wage to perform the role of a manager and lead your employees. Don't adapt to the lower standards of culture. Instead, create a high standard that, when compared to other managers, may seem a little weird.

**Coaching Thoughts – For You and Your Peers**

- After comparing the characteristics of the two kinds of managers, do you agree that the "Weird Managers" really are the good ones? Which kind of manager would you prefer to be? To have as a boss?

- Where did you fall on the "Normal Managers versus Weird Managers" quiz? Are you comfortable with that? If you landed in the "Normal Manager" category, could the fact that you are content where you are be a sign that you need to push yourself to grow more?

- Regardless of where you landed on the quiz, take a moment to make a plan for growth using the characteristics of the "Weird Manager". Try to come up with other characteristics that would fit the "Weird Manager".

# Three Ways to Make Better Decisions

In the midst of the chaos comes yet more work. You're already way overloaded with 20-plus direct reports, and you still have to fill those two open manager positions. You are working 13 hours a day just to keep the fires at bay by providing minimal direction and insight to all those direct reports. Should you just promote that internal candidate who has far less management experience than the job and team requires? At least you'd have boots on the ground to help you manage the everyday fires, and you'd be able to pull you head up a bit from the trees to see more of the forest.

We are constantly faced with decisions, some small and mundane, others far-reaching and complex. The muckiness of decision-making can be caused by the environment, our unique personality, the political storms surrounding us, and the emotional baggage that we carry around from all our life decisions (both good and bad). Dan and Chip Heath's recent book, *Decisive: How to Make Better Choices in Life and Work,* offers up tremendous insight on how our decision-making is disrupted by our overconfidence, biases, and short term emotions.

Here are three tactics you can use to make better decisions.

- **Think AND not OR** – When looking at a decision, most leaders see a decision between two outcomes: this or that, hire the internal candidate or don't. Widen your options by using AND instead, allowing yourself to see multiple tracks: a spectrum of possible combinations.

- **Start Ooching** – Start with some small experiments to test decision paths out a bit. In the words of the Heath brothers, ooching is a combination of "scoot" and "inch". So try ooching forward to gather more data and to gain clarity on what the real decision actually is, or to test out a portion of your decision. You should ooch before taking the full leap. For issue of the internal manager candidate mentioned earlier, can the leader ooch the process by borrowing the manager for 10 hours a week from their current department, testing her out in the role?

- **10-10-10** – Ask yourself, "How will I feel about this decision 10 days from now? 10 months from now? 10 years from now?" This time framing process allows you to gain perspective and add distance so you can emotionally sort through the impact of the decision. You should be able to gain clarity around the internal conflicts which may be impacting your decision process.

Practice some of these techniques with the decisions confronting you today and adjust your trend line of success. You just may make better decisions.

**Coaching Thoughts – For You and Your Peers**

- When was the last time you faced a tough decision? What did you do to make up your mind one way or another? Take a moment to think about how the three tactics outlined here might have helped you in that situation?

- Which of these three tactics for decision making jumps out at you most? Why do you think this is?

- How might you benefit from using all three of these suggestions, rather than just on?

81

# The Slow Fade of a Leader and His Authority

There he sits, the 52-year-old, slightly graying VP. He's in the same seat he sits in every week at the meeting. He's present, but he's not really *here*. He talks, but no one actually listens to what he's saying. He's productive and his team seems to get the minimal work completed, but they aren't a thriving team. What's happened to him, you wonder?

He's in the slow fade season of leadership.

Leaders don't come to work thinking "yes, today I'm going to let my leadership and authority slip just a bit and continue this slow fade of my impact." They come to work each day fighting the battles of politics, striving to meet the goals rolled down from the boss, exerting just enough energy towards employees to keep them feeling that they are engaged, and creating an appearance of productivity by attending 8 meetings and driving through 120 emails.

The irony is that the slow fade of a leader comes from the toll of those exact battles, and from years of pulling energy from the deep crevices of their heart and soul. Each day, a little more is given up to "the man", resulting in something less being left over in the leader. There's not a watershed moment when everything shifts from impactful to not impactful. Sure, your recent performance review says something happened this year in your behaviors, but in reality, those behaviors were always there.

Strong, capable, non-fading leaders have the courage to lead forward. This courage comes from their capability to strive for the prime directive they've set forth as the goal for themselves, their team, and their company (which may or may not align with that of the boss); to

82

ignore all the work that they *could* accomplish, focusing narrowly on those two or three talents which they alone bring to the table for their team or company. A leader who can balance his talents with those of his team will create an enabling environment for success. And low and behold, he will not be entrenched "**in**" the battles but will instead lead his team through them... and keep himself growing as well.

Leaders don't crumble in a day, but each day can be the start of their crumbling. You need to embrace the struggle and to decide today what two or three things only you can do for your team or company. Then focus intently on those gifts.

**Coaching Thoughts – For You and Your Peers**

- Take a moment to think: have you ever felt like you've stopped growing as a leader? Try to think of a specific example.

- What are some things you can do now to prevent yourself from falling from a leader with authority to an ineffective leader?

- Do you know any leaders who are in the slow fade of leadership? How can you enable them to stop sinking?

# The Crucible

*Crucible:* A place or occasion of severe test or trial.

Marine Corp recruits culminate their boot camp training with "The Crucible", a 54 hour strenuous training exercise meant to simulate typical combat situations wherein recruits apply everything they've learned to that point in their training. The "exercise" includes 48 miles of marching while carrying 75 pounds of gear, having limited access to food, being deprived of sleep and having to navigate severe obstacles as a team under battle conditions. Practice Marine Corp style is evidently very real.

How do you practice as a leader? Have you put yourself through the same level of training as Marine recruits by creating a chance to fully experience all the aspects of your leadership role in *live business* conditions before the skills are required? Have you had a crucible training experience?

The capability of a well-trained, practiced leader to act and behave in crystal clear ways, at critical moments in time, can be extremely valuable to a company and to those whom the leader leads. Creating a "live conditions" business leadership boot camp experience akin to the Marines may be difficult and impractical. So, great leaders have figured out that if they invest time each week reflecting deeply upon and situationally assessing their behaviors, they can practice their leadership and at times, create virtual crucible training experiences. This visualization process helps the leaders to see how their behaviors ripple within their team, the organization, their customers and their family and community.

Be reflective, practice leadership and create your virtual crucible training experiences.

## Coaching Thoughts – For You and Your Peers

- How do you practice as a leader? What are some ways to get this practice?

- Have you had a crucible experience? If so, what was it?

# The Power- or Impotence – of Your Leadership Habits

Habits follow a fairly predictable pattern of a cue (or trigger, craving) which enacts a routine to achieve a reward. A habit is the brain's efficient method of decreasing power consumption. Think about personal habits you perform all the time: brushing your teeth, walking, reading a text message after hearing the ding, saying hi to your mom on the phone, backing your car out of a parking spot. Habits can be good for us as well as bad for us, think about the draw of unhealthy food to relieve stress or the debilitating addiction of some drugs. *The Power of Habit: Why We Do What We Do in Life and Business* by Charles Duhigg, is an extremely fascinating and intriguing book which delves into the science of how our brains create these habits and how we together create cultural habits in our organizations.

As a new leader, everything you did was so new to you that you didn't yet have a habit to help you perform at an efficient level.

- How to run your 1<sup>st</sup> team meeting

- What to say to your employee who just did something great

- How to deliver crucial, critical feedback to an employee

- How to delegate work

- How to network with new peers

Now, as a seasoned leader you are much more efficient. You can easily prepare for a meeting as well as know how to stay awake in your 5<sup>th</sup> meeting of the day, you've fired a few employees, you know how to go into autopilot when delivering tough feedback, delegation comes easily, and strategy sessions and long range planning are walks in the park.

Seasoned leaders rely heavily on habits to be as effective as possible in their role. Many of these habits help the leader to be efficient and effective in their roles but sadly many of those habits create dysfunction, unrest and low productivity with teams because the leader is on autopilot. He follows the same course of action he has in similar situations without recognizing the subtle differences in composition of the employee groups and the environment or worse, recognizing the differences but being too lazy or lacking the courage to adjust his routines.

**Coaching Thoughts – For You and Your Peers**

- Which of your leadership habits might be causing more harm than good?

- Do you know anyone who relies too much on habit? Do *you* rely too much on habit? How can you break (or help someone else) break out of their habits?

# Building the Accountable Culture of Your Team

It would be great if employees were more accountable, took initiative, went the extra mile, took responsibility for their own development, were self-motivated not being influenced by the negative behaviors of others and quickly turned failures into lessons learned. Our roles as leaders would be so much easier.

So, ask yourself these questions:

- How do I encourage and support the new ideas people have?

- What do I do when people step up and work "outside their box" to "do the right thing" even if it's not in the "rules"

- What are the behaviors I display that show I encourage and support employees "thinking" rather than just "showing up and filling their seat?"

- What am I doing to elevate the desired behaviors I seek from my employees?

I believe your charge should be: To act consistently in ways that model the values, performance, culture and most importantly, personal responsibility you expect of yourself and within your team and the organization.

**Coaching Thoughts – For You and Your Peers**

To you agree or disagree with "the charge" in the last paragraph?

If a videographer followed you around for a week, what behaviors would the videos reveal? Would you be proud or disturbed?

# Three Ways to Enable Your Boss to Be Great

So you're telling me your boss just isn't the best leader. He has weaknesses and struggles and just isn't as effective as you really need him to be. Maybe it's time for *you* to help him become a better boss. Here are three ways you can invest in your boss to enable him to be great.

- **Serve Him** – What are the things you can do to help your boss be successful in his role? Go deep with your thoughts – beyond the "accomplish all my work" type thoughts – to thoughts regarding what is causing my boss to be less than fantastic? Move beyond being selfish to truly seeking ways to help your boss to be better, energized, excited, thoughtful, strategic, administratively efficient, and charismatic.

- **Speak His Language** – Analyze your and his preferred communication styles. You invest time to think through how best you can communicate with your employees, really trying to make the road a two way street. Invest the same time in understanding the uniqueness of your boss' style and in what ways you can adjust *your* energy, style, approach, and language to elicit the best communication from your boss.

- **Read About Leadership** – Invest in learning about your chosen profession. Read books, articles and blog posts on leadership every week and use the tools, techniques, tips, strategies, methods, approaches with your boss. It may sound counterintuitive at first, but what are the real differences in managing up versus managing down versus managing sideways. The implementation or execution of certain methods will have to be adjusted since your authority and influence differ and the perception of your role by others differs, but otherwise, most of the methods are stakeholder neutral.

**Coaching Thoughts – For You and Your Peers**

- What will you start doing today to adjust the trend line of your boss' performance?

- Do you think that by investing in these efforts, you will also be modeling the behavior you expect from employees? How?

# Three Ways to Lighten Your Leadership Luggage

We all carry around an invisible piece of leadership luggage. Some stagger under the weight of a huge steamer trunk; some lug an old suitcase, bursting at the seams; others shoulder a backpack, ready for the big hike; still others sling a svelte messenger bag casually over one shoulder. Inside each piece of luggage, we find the burdens of the past: the mistakes that seem to never leave our shadow, the what-could've-beens, the voices of less-than-perfect mentors and parents, the life challenges our employees and kids are facing, our leadership insecurities, our lack of knowledge of the best management practices... the list goes on and on. The burden of this luggage can bear down on us, making it difficult to execute swiftly and with purpose.

Great leaders do 3 things in managing their luggage:

- **Recognizing** – Great leaders visualize the luggage they are carrying. They know there is a burden bag that can be filled every minute of every day. They recognize that subconsciously, they are constantly listening to those voices from the past that bring them down. And most importantly, they recognize that they must see, name, and process those burdens in order to maintain a healthy outlook.

- **Cleansing** – Great leaders take time to empty out the contents of their luggage. They sort through the tasks, projects, responsibilities, and other junk so that they can delegate work, eliminate the jumble that's taking up space, and decide to say no to certain things. They capture the learning moments to create wisdom and purge the insecurities. They know that an investment of time for a healthy cleanse will pay huge dividends by allowing them to be lean and agile.

- **Seeing** – Great leaders see what they will do before they do it. They anticipate. They visualize the collision of events and conversations that will require them to pivot and lead well. And since they know exactly what's in their luggage, they can quickly throw any of it off in a moment's notice, sling the messenger bag over their head, and be fully prepared to use all their energy for their team and the situation in which they find themselves. They are a lean, mean, leading machine.

Great leaders aren't necessarily smarter than the rest of us, but they are more agile and mature. They recognize that they need to invest the time and energy to fit their leadership "stuff" in a messenger bag. But what about you? Are you one of those leaders carrying around a huge steamer trunk? If so, maybe it's time for a good cleansing.

**Coaching Thoughts – For You and Your Peers**

- Re-read the descriptions of the different types of leadership luggage. What kind of bag are you toting around?

- Have you ever struggled with the burden of your leadership luggage? What are some actionable steps you can take to get rid of some of your extra "stuff"?

# The Critical Flaw of Leaders Leading Leaders

There comes a point in time when leaders begin to lead other leaders. They have several people below them who are guiding teams or departments of their own, and they can see the breadth of their empire spread out before them, with all their resources working together to achieve the goals set forth at the last leadership team retreat.

But what is really going on within these teams? Is everyone totally aligned around the goals? Are the employees working diligently? Are they fully engaged and giving all of their *discretionary energy*?

What tends to happen to leaders as they move up the ladder is that they forget the most basic of premises of leadership: relationships are built one employee at a time. Leading well requires that you go back to the basics at every turn and build (or rebuild) relationships, one person at a time. It is through these relationships that you will earn the right to be a person's leader. You will receive their permission to be led.

As these relationships form, you are weaving the fabric of the culture of an organization. Each relationship builds upon the others until ideally, you reach a critical *tipping point* where the culture of your team, department, or organization has tremendous momentum. And it's at exactly this point that great leaders separate themselves from average leaders. Average leaders feel good about this initial momentum and slack off, assuming the leaders below them will continue to build relationships. Great leaders stay in man-to-man formation and continue to build the one-to-one relationships even after the tipping point is reached. And when it comes to great leadership, this makes all the difference.

**Coaching Thoughts – For You and Your Peers**

- Have you forgotten that you need permission from your employees in order to lead them?

    o Are there certain relationships that you could/should invest more time?

- What does this statement mean to you: "Leading well requires that you go back to the basics at every turn."?

# The Echoes of Leadership

A toddler is amazed by the sound of their voice echoing off the walls of a large, empty room. I'm amazed by the echo heard down a valley from a high cliff. The sound reverberates, seeming to go on forever.

The leadership voice of a good leader is heard in the hearts and heads of those they've had the privilege to lead, much like these echoes. The simple phrases, meaningful stories, and short video clips of behaviors and interactions reverberate to guide us. These echoes help us to balance the endless, daily workload with the broader purpose of why we are here. They direct us to make difficult decisions, to engage more deeply, and to be patient yet again with that communication-challenged coworker.

These echoes are motivating, demanding, inspirational, consoling, critical, and comforting. They act as sign posts for us as we walk each day through our work life. And while these echoes can be singular in the phrases said or the behaviors exhibited, their tremendous power comes when the echoes align – words plus behaviors – into a reverberating combination that is extremely impactful.

The echoes of great leaders are heard not only today but again and again in the hearts and heads of employees for decades. As a leader, you have the opportunity every day to create these reverberations.

**Coaching Thoughts – For You and Your Peers**

- What "echoes" from others have been particularly impactful to you?

- What echoes are you producing for your employees, and are they echoes you would like to last a lifetime?

# Leaders Need "Me" Time with Their Boss

When I was a young manager working in Washington DC, my boss at the time began a certain tradition. Each week, she walked with me from our office, to and around the White House, and back again. This 20-minute walk was spent talking about the hows and whats of managing my former peers and, more importantly, laying the ground work for the why behind leadership. At the time, the walks were just a nice way to get out of the office and talk about work. In hindsight, however, I see how truly valuable those consistent, short conversations were in building foundational leadership perspective.

Sadly, too many leaders are not meeting with their bosses on a regular basis. Excuses abound, and most often it is simply that "we're just too busy to get the time together". And maybe you're relieved that you don't have to spend time with the boss. Maybe you aren't used to getting feedback, or you lack the self-confidence to maturely filter the feedback.

But in order to grow as a leader, you need to make sure your boss is meeting with you a minimum of at least once every 2 weeks. If you can get 15 to 18 minutes, fantastic. If time is so precious that you can't spare that much, focus on finding 9 minutes for the catch-up. Make your agenda consistent during those 9 minutes and focus on two items: one leadership challenge you've had in the last week, and one positive leadership behavior you've exhibited.

Granted, your boss should be modeling great leadership and making sure the ongoing feedback sessions are happening. But ultimately, you're the one who needs the face time with your boss, and you're the one who needs the opportunity to gain insight and situational perspective regarding your leadership decisions and behaviors. So it's up to you to make sure you are getting it.

97

Is your boss an idiot? Perhaps… but so what? Feedback is feedback. What a great opportunity for you to practice your patience and communication skills! If you make an effort to receive regular feedback, at the very least you'll see behaviors that you will make sure not to repeat with your employees. And if you look really hard, you might even find a seed of wisdom.

So be different: be a "do as I do" leader, not a "do as I say" leader.

**Coaching Thoughts – For You and Your Peers**

- After reading this, what are you going to do to become a leader who gives and receives good feedback?

- What do you think of the last paragraph? What other frustrating situations do you find yourself in that, seen in a positive light, can become great opportunities?

# Tripwires: The Key to Breaking the Autopilot Cycle

Rock stars and celebrities often have eccentric requirements for their pre-gig preparation rooms. The famous band Van Halen had a clause in their contract that specifically said they wanted bowls of M&Ms backstage, but that all the brown ones must be removed. Seems ridiculous. But there was a method to lead band member David Lee Roth's madness. He was setting up what's called a tripwire; that is, something that will snap us to attention when a decision needs to be made.

The band had a tremendously difficult and complex stage setup for their performances, and most often the tractor trailers would arrive at the performance venues well ahead of the band. Local stagehands would have to follow the setup instructions provided in the contract exactly, because an improper setup could cause major problems during the performance, as well as potential injury to band members.

Upon his arrival, Roth would casually walk into the private band area and look for the M&M bowls. If he saw brown M&Ms, he knew right away that the local stagehands and staff had not read and followed all the instructions in the contract, and would immediately call for a full check of the stage setup. The brown M&Ms were his tripwire.

Leaders often run on autopilot, repeating behaviors – habits – as they go through meetings day after day, week after week, and month after month. Since they're on autopilot, they often miss key opportunities for decision making. Tripwires can be used to set a threshold or deadline that, when hit, requires a decision. Here are a couple of examples:

- A probationary period for a new hire sets a tripwire for you to make the "stay or go" decision.

99

- A "two-employee-complaint" tripwire signals that it's time for you to have a conversation with that leadership-challenged supervisor.

- A goal in your performance review that you've copied and pasted from last 3 years acts as a tripwire to see if your boss is really reading your self-review.

- Giving your administrative assistant the "permission to fire status". This tripwire means she can give you direct feedback regarding your stupid comments at a staff meeting, etc.

- Committing to a quarterly lunch with your career mentor that requires you to take inventory of how you're progressing with your broad leadership development.

- An auto reminder on the $22^{nd}$ day of the month to take a 1 hour retreat the next day to plan the next month's activities to focus on that Quad 2 work.

Use tripwires to startle yourself, force a decision point, and awaken your perspective. Party like a rock star or lead like a legend: either way, just make sure to have a simple yet eccentric tripwire to keep things honest.

### Coaching Thoughts – For You and Your Peers

- Have you ever felt yourself running on autopilot? What situations do you tend to "zone out" in most?

- Think of a time that you would have benefitted from having a tripwire set up? What could have acted as a tripwire in that situation?

- Which of the suggested tripwires did you like the best? Pick at least two and try them out.

# Leading Leaders

#Leadwell

# Becoming the Leader Who the Leader You Are Looking for Is Looking For

We desire to be led by leaders who are fully engaged with us, fully supportive of our growth, completely in tune with our personality gyrations, mature in their patience and perspective of our season in life, insightful to our motivational triggers, and proud of our effort to accomplish and achieve. We can see what we want for ourselves in a leader while we're the followers. We recognize the ways in which a good leader would positively impact us.

But here's the rub: The leaders we aspire to be led by are looking for protégés, team members, and young leaders who are *already* "that type of leader". So while you may look ahead to a point in time when you'll lead in better/different ways, you are actually missing the point that you must lead in those ways *now*.

Your present is the past of your future. Your management behaviors today will be the behaviors on which you look back in the future. How will that "backward glance" appear to you? Will you be proud of your behaviors, decisions and actions? Will that past – which is your current present – have been your best work as a manager? For example, will that minor performance issue you have with an employee today- the one you hesitate to confront- be one of the obvious sign posts you are now using to develop the performance improvement plan or justification for termination? If you had addressed that issue at the proper time, would the employee's performance trend line have changed?

The leader you want to be led by is looking for a leader who would've addressed that issue in the present. Is your lack of management performance now because you did not become a better manager in the past?

The hard coaching advice is this: behave as a great manager now. Start today, and you will become that great leader. The easy excuse of "no one trained me to be a great manager" allows you to play the victim. Great managers, leaders, and people take ownership of their own development and find a way to get trained up.

So, are you becoming the leader who the leader you are looking for is looking for? You need to become that leader today so that when the leader you are looking for looks for the leader you want to be, you are already that leader.

**Coaching Thoughts – For You and Your Peers**

- Who is the "ideal leader" that you look up to? What distinguishes them from the not-so-great leaders you know? Take an honest look at yourself: which one does your leadership behavior match more closely?

- Think about this phrase: "Your management behaviors today will be the behaviors on which you look back in the future. How will that 'backward glance' appear to you?" Are there certain situations that you've been avoiding? If not addressed, how might they come back to haunt you?

- There is always room to grow. What are some actionable steps you can take now to "train yourself up" to become the kind of ideal leader you'd want to have? What new leadership habits could you implement?

# Three Ways We Fail Young Leaders

Generation after generation of leaders have followed the same path: get thrown into the position to take over leading their former peers, spend 10 or so years guessing at what they're supposed to do as a manager, and then start attending leadership development programs which attempt to educate them on the effective ways to manage and lead.

Young leaders, our millennials between 25 and 34 years old, are the future of our companies and organizations. Consider these three ways we limit our leaders and their potential for impact.

1. **We trust our greatest assets with those who are not trained.** The young leader is pulled from the ranks of her team to take on the supervisory or team lead role for 5 to 8 of her peers. We entrust the engagement, productivity and retention of our "company's greatest asset" with someone whose depth of management experience would entail a single bullet on the second page of a leader's resume twice her age. We expect all sorts of professionals — doctors, lawyers, teachers, engineers — to be educated and apprenticed in their craft before being left alone. Guiding and educating young leaders in the art of managing and leading others before, or in conjunction with, taking on these roles, creates a tremendous return on investment given the asset they are charged with managing.

2. **We seek and reward bad habits**. Young leaders build and refine bad habits as they are left on their own for 8 or 10 years before being *entitled* to receive leadership development training. Conservatively, organizations spend 3 to 4 times as much money per leader on training and coaching programs for experienced leaders as compared to money spent on young leaders. Average, merely adequate tenured leaders are asked to

105

mentor young leaders and model the behaviors that will make them successful in leadership. But are these habits ones we truly want our young leaders to emulate? Investing in the leadership development of young leaders so they create the good habits will allow these leaders to learn their craft early, practice often, and build their competence.

3. **We don't try to understand young leaders.** Generational misunderstanding is a constant throughout history. Every generation worries about the capability of succeeding generations to lead our society forward. We are blessed with a vast number of studies, books and articles telling us how the millennial generation thinks and acts in ways that are unique from previous generations. We know they are more tech-savvy, more collaborative, more accepting of diversity and more innovative. We know they are better educated in total and continue to educate themselves daily; they are lifelong learners. We should encourage and enable young leaders, and leaders to be, to develop peer coaching/development circles that would allow for seemingly unstructured learning. We should seed the collision of thought and practice to enable a future direction.

It's wonderful that organizations are reviewing succession plans, developing depth charts and identifying their high potentials. I'm confident the plans are thorough and look good. But who's helping that young leader who is wrestling with how to have a difficult conversation with one of her employees and doesn't even know there's a difference between counseling and coaching conversations?

**Coaching Thoughts – For You and Your Peers**

- Take a moment to think: have you seen any of the three bullet points happening in your organization? What can you do about it?

- Have you ever attended some kind of leadership training program? At what point in your career did this occur? Was it beneficial, or would you have liked it to come at a different time?

# She Came In Knowing

A 52-year-old vice president struggles to keep his job. While "successful" throughout his career, it seems he now lacks the leadership capability to adequately enable his team of 55-plus folks to achieve basic success. He also lacks the introspection to see that his domineering, "take-the-hill-at-all-costs" style has disengaged him from not only his team, but also many peers and his boss. What he perceives as the talent that got him here will ultimately be the cause of his downfall. If he had only had the opportunity to learn how to lead early in his career, maybe things would have turned out differently.

Every so often, a company gets lucky and promotes a young leader who is technically adept and happens to have had both the life experiences and decent mentors to guide the development of the soft side of leadership. She came to the company with a treasure chest full of talent, though likely the company has no idea of exactly the true value of that talent.

- She came to the company knowing how she impacts others with her results-oriented communications style.

- She came in knowing how to take feedback constructively and, conversely, how to provide timely, constructive feedback.

- She came in knowing what truly motivates her beyond the standard triggers of shallow corporate recognition and hours in the office.

- She came in knowing conflict more often signals miscommunication and misunderstood expectations rather than a dislike of others.

- She came in wanting to make things better while achieving great success.

- She came in knowing how to disarm the bullies and lift up the dreams of her peers.

- She came in knowing time invested in introspection pays huge dividends in future behavior choices.

Building leaders requires time and energy spent educating young leaders on the science of managing others and on the art of influencing. There are no short cuts, and there are no special pills. You have to invest in building management intelligence and leadership capability and, most importantly, you must provide above-average mentorship to these young, aspiring leaders. It is in this last area, above-average mentorship, which companies seem to be the most lacking. Because they have grown and built merely average leaders who lack leadership maturity in their own work, they have no one to adequately provide the model of leadership young leaders should follow.

**Coaching Thoughts – For You and Your Peers**

- Think back to the 52-year-old vice president and the countless leaders who worked for him throughout his career mentioned at the beginning of this Leadership Learning Moment. How has the company limited their effectiveness and growth as leaders as they try to follow his model? And what has the impact been on the company's leadership capacity?

- What can you do to help the leaders under you so that they *don't* end up like the 52-year-old vice president? What can you do for yourself?

# How Interim Assignments Can Grow Leadership Capacity

The departure of a high level leader from an organization creates a vacuum of leadership. In rare circumstances a company actually has an up-to-date and implementable succession plan. But for most companies, the succession plan notebook sits right next to the dust covered copy of the strategic plan on the middle shelf of the tall bookcase. So, basically, there are two options to pursue:

1. **Safe But Short Sighted** – Assign the departing leader's responsibilities to a combination of peers and the boss or a single peer or subordinates within the business function.

2. **Investing in the Future** – Move a high performing, lower ranking leader from a different business function into the role for an interim assignment.

The radical approach of option #2 appears on the surface as far too risky and disruptive to the organization. The interim leader will be limited in functional knowledge, will be temporarily leading peers, will leave a huge hole in his/her home department and will need support and mentoring to be successful. But the disruption might well be exactly what the organization needs to create collisions of talented people that inspire/encourage updated approaches which will:

- Spark innovation.

- Realign the energy of relationships.

- Challenge staid productivity.

- Build leadership wisdom with real job experience.

Let your mind wonder for a moment on the following interim assignments.

- An IT leader to a Human Resources role

- A Finance leader to Sales

- A Human Resources leader to Manufacturing or IT

- A Customer Services leader to Finance

- A Manufacturing Foreman/Leader to Customer Service

Stretching the growth of your internal leaders by moving a high potential to the interim role and increasing the roles of those the high potential leaves in leadership behind her/him increases the leadership capacity within the organization. And a depth of leadership capacity is a defining success factor for teams, organizations, and companies.

Have the courage to invest in and grow your leaders to reap the long term rewards of broad and deep leadership capacity.

**Coaching Thoughts – For You and Your Peers**

- What do you think of this interim assignment idea? Can you see it working for (and benefitting) your organization? Remember, it takes courage.

- What do you think this statement means: "...a depth of leadership capacity is a defining success factor for teams, organizations, and companies."? Do you agree with it?

# The Three Things That Trip Up New Leaders

Walking up a trail in the Adirondacks with a 50-pound pack while staring at the majestic scenery creates the prime opportunity to catch your toe on the root in the path and tumble forward. Doing it twice in a matter of 15 minutes… well, that just feels stupid.

New leaders – and forgetful seasoned leaders – tend to make classic mistakes in their positions. They meander down the path, staring at the sky, not seeing the tree roots that will trip them up. These "tree roots" are found in three areas of leadership.

- **Misjudging the Source of Authority** – Newer leaders tend to misjudge from where, exactly, their authority is derived. Authority is a magical quality that, when used correctly, yields tremendous power to influence others and get things done. Conversely, when used incorrectly or naively, new leaders struggle with a lack of engagement and respect from their employees. Review these 5 types of authority and think about which would be most effective in different situations.

- **Ineffective Investment of Time** – Leaders have the opportunity to spend their time doing technical work, interacting with humans, and/or conceptually thinking forward. The challenges lay in the tension between doing what's comfortable (the technical stuff) while shying away from the human aspects and never "finding" the time to think conceptually. Successful leaders learn quickly to invest their time in the human and conceptual buckets more than technical buckets, allowing them to lead rather than react.

- **Finding Their Place** – New leaders struggle with finding their place in this new world of management. First, though they recognize that there are relationships which need to be built with new peers, there's this confusing, political mine field, and crossing that can feel like trying to navigate Baltimore with a map of Chicago. Second, there's the fun of figuring out how to tweak relationships with former peers who are now employees. Should they still go to lunch? What about happy hour? Finally, where exactly should they sit during the big, bad management staff meeting they've never attended before?

Great leaders are built over time as they get up off the ground and study the root in the path that just tripped them up. They learn to examine what happened, why, and who was impacted in what ways. They mature over time using this information to adjust their behaviors. They seek other good leaders from whom they can learn and to whom they can teach. And they try like heck to not trip over the same root twice.

## Coaching Thoughts – For You and Your Peers

- Think back to a time when you made one of these "classic mistakes".

    o What happened?

    o How was it resolved?

    o How can remembering this help you handle things when your team members slip up in the same ways?

- What other "tree roots" have caused you to trip up in your walk as a leader?

# Five Ways to Apprentice a Young Leader

Young leaders want to grow quickly to become effective managers and business leaders and while companies like to leverage these resources as soon as possible, a concerted effort to invest in building these leaders would be more appropriate. Young leaders desperately need to learn the craft of management and the art of leadership which takes time, living through experiences, making mistakes and practicing good leadership behaviors. Ideally companies would create an apprenticeship approach which would provide a coordinated approach to driving young leaders through a series of assignments and interactions to strengthen their people acumen, build wisdom, create business perspective and develop broad communication skills.

Here are 5 ways to apprentice a young leader.

1. Move the supervisor to manage a similarly sized team in a different business function for one year.

2. Send the administrative manager out in the field with a successful sales rep for 8 weeks on the road with customers.

3. Allow one or two young leaders to sit in on senior leadership meetings to observe how senior leaders interact, debate, and resolve conflict while traversing significant and diverse business issues.

4. Setup an apprentice circle with several young leaders with whom you will meet every other month for a year. Everyone reads a book for each meeting and prepares a one page summary of the book assigned bringing copies of the summary for others in the group. Invest 90 minutes to 2 hours discussing the book, its application to life at work and in general, and real

114

life stories of leading in the trenches. Here's a list of books to consider.

- *The Five Dysfunctions of a Team: A Leadership Fable* by Patrick Lencioni

- *Poke the Box* by Seth Godin

- *First, Break All the Rules: What the World's Greatest Managers Do Differently* by Marcus Buckingham

- *Team of Rivals: The Political Genius of Abraham Lincoln* by Doris Kearns Goodwin

- *The 5 Levels of Leadership: Proven Steps to Maximize Your Potential* by John Maxwell

- *Great Leaders Grow: Becoming a Leader for Life* by Ken Blanchard

- *Tribes: We Need You to Lead Us* by Seth Godin

- *Outliers: The Story of Success* by Malcolm Gladwell

- *Death by Meeting: A Leadership Fable...About Solving the Most Painful Problem in Business* by Patrick Lencioni

5. Build trusted relationships. Talk to them. Take them out to lunch or breakfast and really talk with them about their life, their experiences at work, the wisdom they are gaining, and their struggles. Build a trusted relationship that will open the door to allow you to provide deep, constructive insight.

All companies desire a bench of strong leaders from whom they can choose successors for key roles. Successful companies build their bench.

**Coaching Thoughts – For You and Your Peers**

- What will you do this year to begin building your bench?

- Are you a young leader seeking apprenticeship? Or do you know any? What experiences do you think would help to build your/their leadership capacity?

# # #

# **About The Author**

#Leadwell

# Michael Holland

Michael Holland unravels the mysteries of leadership. Michael is a professional executive coach and trusted advisor to executives who seek to become better leaders and build cohesive teams. Michael's wisdom and insight are the product of 30 years of leadership experience and an uncanny, natural ability to perceive the questions that need to be asked.

Michael founded Bishop House Consulting, Inc. in 1999 to provide organizational leadership expertise and team development services to companies experiencing dynamic change. Michael has provided distinguished executive coaching services to well over 300 leaders in organizations, ranging from start-ups to multi-billion dollar corporations. Michael earned his MBA from the University of Baltimore and is the author of *Leadership Learning Moments*, a weekly inspiration – or reminder – regarding the critical role leaders play in the lives of employees.

In addition to his role leading Bishop House Consulting, Michael serves on the Area Committee for Young Life Capital Region, invests his time and energy instigating men who seek more purpose in life, is a member of Grace Chapel of Clifton Park, and is active in the Burnt Hills, NY community where he lives with his wife and their three kids.

LinkedIn: mikeatbishophouse

Instigating Men Blog: www.michaelsholland.com

Email: mike@bishophouse.com

Twitter: @mikehollandatbh

#Leadwell

# Bishop House Consulting, Inc.

Bishop House Consulting is the premier leadership development and organizational consulting firm working with companies in New York's Capital Region and Tech Valley. Founded by Michael Holland in 1999, the firm has grown steadily, maintaining trusted, long term relationships with clients. Bishop House coaches, trainers and consultants are well regarded as thought leaders in developing effective executives and managers, building cohesive teams, and navigating organizational change.

Bishop House Consulting excels at building both leadership capability within all levels of leaders and the leadership capacity of organizations. The firm works with leaders through training programs and coaching projects, focusing on building from the core out. We believe that creating deep self-awareness of one's leadership style enables opportunities to build trusted relationships, which in turn allows for the formation of cohesive teams. We help leaders seek those keystone behaviors in their core management routines, which can be adjusted to allow for initial shifts in their leadership behavior. With continued practice, these behaviors become effective leadership habits, resulting in more effective leaders and greater leadership capacity within the organization.

Bishop House Consulting helps leaders, teams and companies increase their effectiveness through exploration of personal communication styles and team dynamics with *Everything DiSC*® assessments and training solutions. Bishop House Consulting is an independent Authorized Distributor of *DiSC*® products and services.

www.BishopHouse.com

*DiSC*® *is a registered trademark of Inscape Publishing, Inc.*

121